WHAT ON EARTH CAN WE DO?

by Emily Sper

JUMP | PRESS

NEWTONVILLE

We live on the planet Earth.

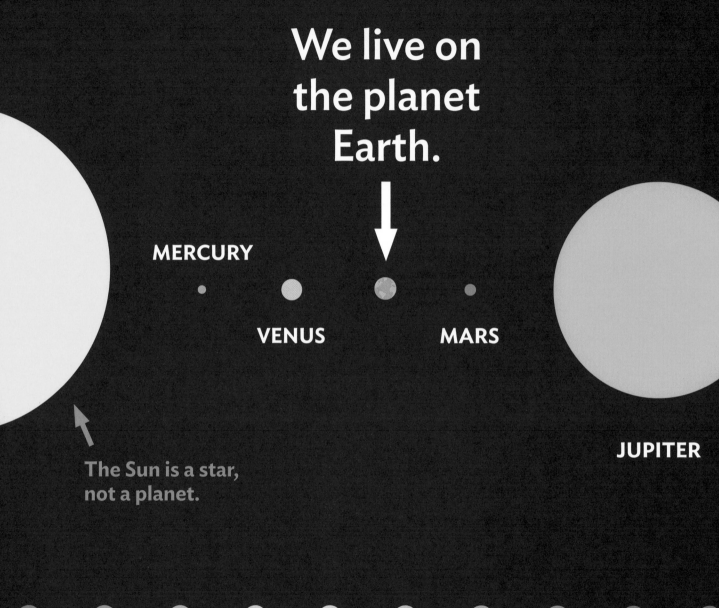

MERCURY

VENUS

MARS

JUPITER

The Sun is a star, not a planet.

Planets

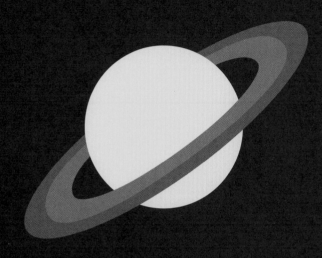

SATURN

URANUS

NEPTUNE

RAIN FOREST

OCEAN

POLAR ICE CAP

DESERT

Earth has many special places. How can we protect them?

Make less garbage.

We don't want garbage to ruin the places we love.

Repair toys instead of buying new ones.

Reuse an empty box to store your treasures.

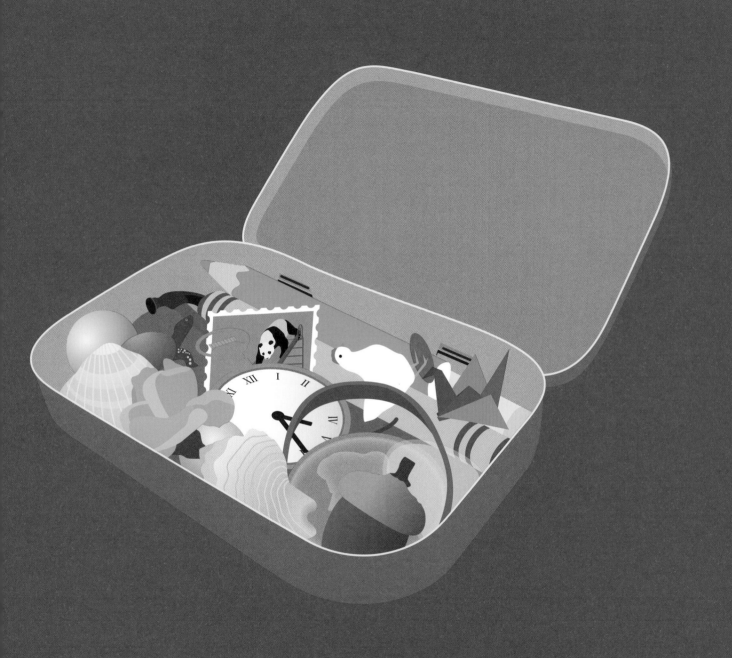

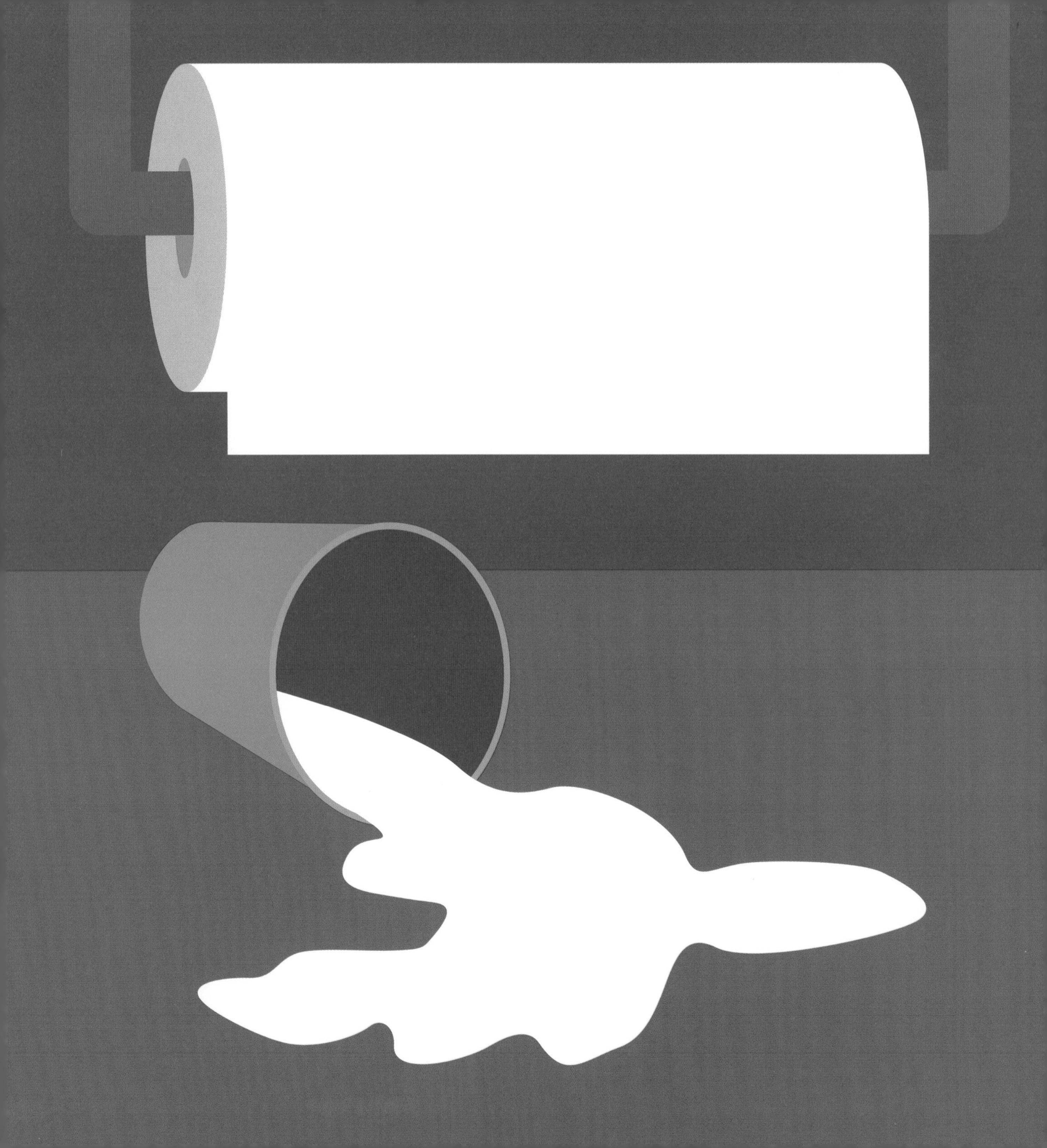

Use only one paper towel to clean up a spill, unless you really need to use two.

Even better, use a sponge or cloth rag.

When you go shopping, take your own bag.

Then you won't bring a plastic bag home. And take your own water bottle, in case you get thirsty.

Recycle.

Some garbage can be broken down and made into something new. Did you know plastic bottles can be turned into yarn to make a carpet or sweater?

Planet Earth News

Today   Meadowlark Pond

Kids Changing the World

All around the world, kids are convincing their parents to recycle:

- **NEWSPAPERS, MAGAZINES, CARDBOARD, AND JUNK MAIL**
- **ALUMINUM FOIL**
- **ALUMINUM, STEEL, AND TIN CANS**
- **JUICE BOXES**
- **MILK CARTONS**
- **PLASTIC BAGS**
- **PLASTIC BOTTLES, CONTAINERS, AND PACKAGING**
- **GLASS BOTTLES AND JARS**

Kids are teaching their parents to take shorter showers, travel on public transportation or bike to work, set up a compost bin, and use energy-efficient light bulbs.

Kids say "no" to pesticides to keep the grass green and "no" to cleaning products with toxic chemicals.

Kids say "yes" to organic fruits and vegetables that are grown in clean soil and not sprayed with pesticides.

Kids say "yes" to local farms and small gardens.

PAPER →

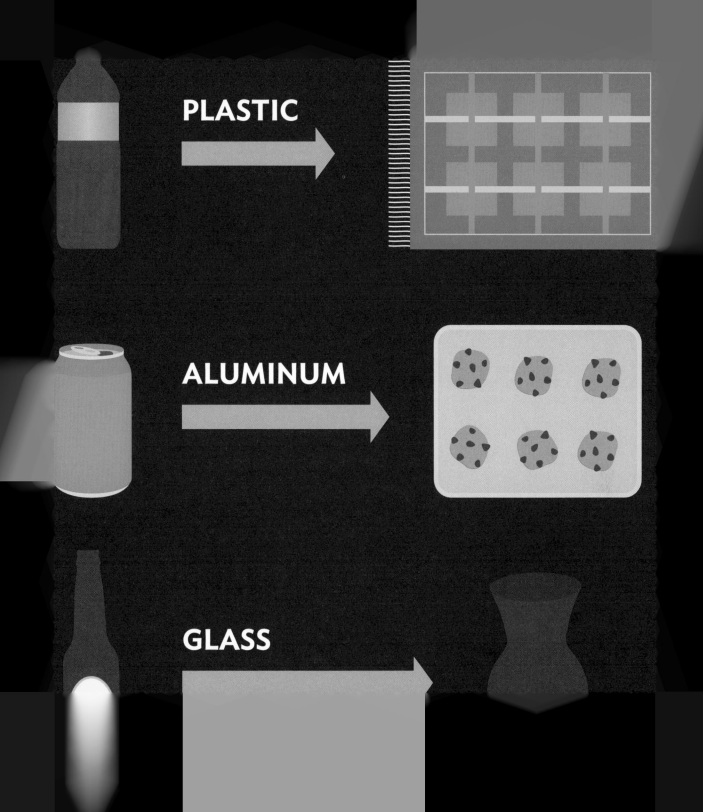

PLASTIC

ALUMINUM

GLASS

If your supermarket has a recycling center, take clean plastic bags and empty drink bottles and cans for recycling.

GLASS BOTTLES

PLASTIC BOTTLES

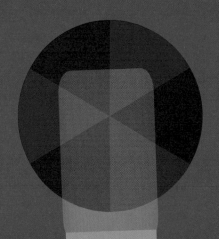

ALUMINUM CANS

Put other plastics, glass, aluminum, steel, tin, and paper in recycling bins for your town to collect. In some towns, you may have to take recycling to the dump. If you live in an apartment house, look for shared bins.

In your town, do you put paper in one bin and plastics and other recycling in another bin?

Or do you put everything in one cart?

Compost.

Put food scraps in a compost bin. Then worms, insects, bacteria, and fungi get to work—they turn the food scraps into rich soil that helps plants grow.

Worm Café

BREAKFAST
Fruit Peels & Pits

LUNCH
Vegetable Scraps

SUPPER
Eggshells

DESSERT
Dead Leaves

Compost Bin, USA

COMPOST BIN

Plant a tree.

Trees help clean the air we breathe.

Turn off lights when you leave a room.

Don't waste electricity.

Turn off the faucet while brushing your teeth.

Don't waste water.

We can make a difference.

Planet Earth News

Kids Changing the World

All around the world, kids are convincing their parents to recycle:

- **NEWSPAPERS, MAGAZINES, CARDBOARD, AND JUNK MAIL**
- **ALUMINUM FOIL**
- **ALUMINUM, STEEL, AND TIN CANS**
- **JUICE BOXES**
- **MILK CARTONS**
- **PLASTIC BAGS**
- **PLASTIC BOTTLES, CONTAINERS, AND PACKAGING**
- **GLASS BOTTLES AND JARS**

Kids are teaching their parents to take shorter showers, travel on public transportation or bike to work, set up a compost bin, and use energy-efficient light bulbs.

Kids say "no" to pesticides to keep the grass green and "no" to cleaning products with toxic chemicals.

Kids say "yes" to organic fruits and vegetables that are grown in clean soil and not sprayed with pesticides.

Kids say "yes" to local farms and small gardens.

The animals thank you for helping to protect Earth.

And now for some big words and ideas.

ELECTRICITY AND FOSSIL FUELS

Electricity is a form of power.

Most electricity is made from heating fossil fuels—coal, oil, or natural gas—found deep underground.

CARBON DIOXIDE

When we burn fossil fuels, a gas called carbon dioxide is released into the atmosphere— the air surrounding Earth.

Most cars burn fossil fuels. Buses, trains, and airplanes run on fossil fuels, too. And fossil fuels are used to produce much of our food and everything else.

GLOBAL WARMING

The more fossil fuels we burn, the warmer our planet gets.

If there's too much carbon dioxide in the atmosphere, the sun's heat and light energy get trapped close to the earth.

Oceans and land warm up, which changes our climate—how hot, rainy, or windy it is. We call this "climate change."

TREES

Trees help us to live. They take carbon dioxide out of the air and turn it into oxygen for us to breathe. They take harmful chemicals out of the soil, too.

And leafy trees give us shade on a sunny day. Fruit and nut trees give us food to eat, year after year.

Trees help, but there is still too much carbon dioxide in the atmosphere. We need to burn less fossil fuel!

WATER

People, animals, and plants need water to live.

If we use too much water, there will be none left. Then we'll have to wait for rainwater to fill up our reservoirs—deep lakes where water is stored. This will take a long time.

RENEWABLE ENERGY

Energy is power. It is what makes cars, computers, and even our bodies work.

Our bodies get energy from the food we eat.

Most cars and computers run on energy from fossil fuels, but there are other sources of energy.

WIND TURBINE

We can capture energy from the sun and wind.

Solar power, which comes from the sun, and wind power don't get used up — they are renewable. And, unlike fossil fuels, they don't hurt Earth.

SOLAR PANELS

Let's protect Earth!

Make less garbage.

Repair.

Reuse.

Recycle.

Compost.

Plant a tree.

Don't waste electricity or water.

What will you do?

Dedicated in loving memory to my parents, Rose and Roy Sper,
who chose to bring me up in a house surrounded by trees.

Special thanks to Jenny Barber, Tom Brown, Adena Cohen-Bearak, Phoebe Cushman, Linda Falken, Bernette Ford, Jane Gerver, Ellie Goldberg, Laurie Goldman, Orit Kent, Derek Pieper, Eve Pranis, Amy Rosenthal, Liz Rosenthal, Debbie Schermer, Jane Sper, Chagit Steiner, and Edie Weinberg.

ISBN 978-0-9754902-7-3

Printed in China

First printing, July 2016

All of our papers are sourced from managed forests and renewable resources.